· TRUE HAUNTINGS ·

BATTLEFIELD
GHOSTS

TRUE HAUNTINGS

BATTLEFIELD GHOSTS

DINAH WILLIAMS

SCHOLASTIC PRESS / NEW YORK

Copyright © 2021 by Dinah Dunn

All rights reserved. Published by Scholastic Press, an imprint of Scholastic Inc., *Publishers since 1920.* SCHOLASTIC, SCHOLASTIC PRESS, and associated logos are trademarks and/or registered trademarks of Scholastic Inc.

Library of Congress Cataloging-in-Publication Data available

ISBN 978-1-338-35586-4

10 9 8 7 6 5 4 3 2 1   21 22 23 24 25

Printed in the U.S.A.   40

First edition, August 2021

Book design by Kay Petronio

To Cathy Hemming,
for always going to battle for me.

· CONTENTS ·

INTRODUCTION

"War, at the best, is terrible, and this war of ours, in its magnitude and in its duration, is one of the most terrible."

—*Abraham Lincoln*

On battlefields, death is everywhere you look. In the chaos of gunfire and bombs, soldiers are often shot, blown up, or trampled in the rush. Sometimes there are so many dead, the bodies can't be found or buried amid the horrors.

Yet what makes battlefields so terrible also makes them an ideal place to find ghosts. When death comes unexpectedly, like in war, people may not know or accept that they are dead. Their spirits become stuck where they died, doomed to repeat the final moments of their lives. As many battlefields are now memorials to fallen soldiers, they are often haunted by these poor ghosts. This is especially true on the anniversary of the event because that's when the memory is strongest.

Ghost hunters have tried to gather evidence of these

ghosts' existence, such as images of spirits in photographs and sounds on audiotape. But often the only sources we have are what people have seen or felt in a particular place. That is the basis for many of the stories in this book.

Battlefield Ghosts is filled with many tragic tales of soldiers who lost their lives, as well as some of the most haunted places on Earth. You'll meet ancient spirits that

The 1862 Battle of Antietam took place during the American Civil War mainly on either side of a sunken road between farms in Maryland. In four hours, more than five thousand soldiers died in the area now known as the Bloody Lane. After the battle, there were so many corpses that you couldn't walk without stepping on one. Ghost sightings there are common, with the weirdest story reported by some Maryland schoolboys in 1982. They heard men singing what sounded like the "Fa la la la la" from the Christmas carol "Deck the Halls." They didn't know that in that exact spot, the Irish Brigade had charged into the fight. Their Gaelic battle cry sounds a lot like "Deck the Halls." More than 60 percent of the brigade were killed that day.

drag ships down to the depths, and other ghosts who are just looking for a light for their cigarette. They haunt islands in the middle of the vast ocean and small rural towns where battles once raged. What these ghosts have in common is that death caught them by surprise, took their lives without warning, and left their spirits trapped here on Earth, ready for you to discover.

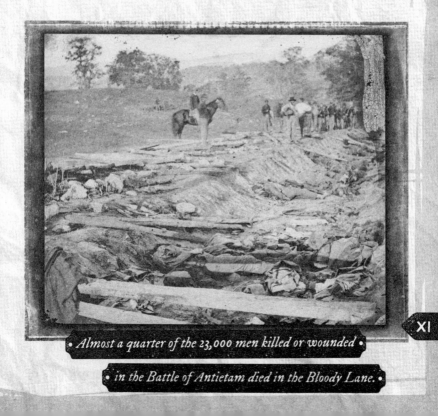

Almost a quarter of the 23,000 men killed or wounded in the Battle of Antietam died in the Bloody Lane.

1

DEMON FIRE

Japanese fishermen are careful about what they catch along the Kanmon Straits, which separate two of the country's main islands. They try to avoid the Heikegani crabs, whose shells bear the eerie image of a samurai mask. According to Japanese folklore, the crabs contain the souls of the Heike samurai warriors killed in the straits at the Battle of Dan-no-ura in AD 1185.

This naval battle took place between the fleet of the Heike (also known as the Taira clan), led by the child emperor Antoku, and the Minamoto (or Genji clan), led by Minamoto no Yoshitsune. Initially the two sides were somewhat evenly matched, with archers raining arrows onto opposing ships. Eventually the Heike began to surround and board the Minamoto ships, leading to vicious hand-to-hand fighting between the samurai warriors.

Then the tide turned. A Heike general defected to the Minamoto and attacked the Heike from the rear. He also told the Minamoto which ship held the six-year-old emperor, who was traveling with his grandmother.

When the Heike commander Tomomori realized they were going to be defeated, he tied an anchor to his waist and threw himself into the sea, choosing to take his own life rather than die at the hands of the enemy. Many Heike followed him, including the emperor's grandmother. She grabbed the young emperor Antoku, saying, "In the depths of the sea, we have a capital." She dragged him to his death on the ocean floor.

These abrupt and terrible deaths have led to many sightings of angry and vengeful samurai ghosts along the Kanmon Straits.

Dan-no-ura was the final battle in the Genpei War (1180–1185), a civil war in Japan between the Taira and Minamoto clans. This led to a military leadership of the country by Minamoto no Yoritomo and the rise of the samurai.

Minamoto no Yoshitsune was considered one of the greatest samurai of his generation. In one fight on the Gojo Ohashi Bridge, he bested a renowned warrior monk named Benkei. When he lost, Benkei swore his eternal allegiance to Yoshitsune. During the Genpei War, Yoshitsune aided his half brother Minamoto no Yoritomo, who went on to rule Japan once the war was over.

The massive monk Benkei challenged Yoshitsune to a sword fight. When he was defeated, Benkei loyally followed Yoshitsune for the rest of his days.

Yoritomo began to worry that his half brother was becoming too powerful and too popular. He decided that Yoshitsune was a threat to his rule and must die. Before his brother's soldiers could kill him, Yoshitsune fled with the loyal Benkei by his side. They boarded a ship to take them to safety across Dan-no-ura Bay.

Legend says that after the ship set sail, a weird fog appeared, blocking out the sun. Huge waves rocked the boat and the winds let out an angry wail. Looking out into the water, Yoshitsune realized that the disturbance wasn't caused by a storm. In the waves he saw the ghostly hands of

Yoshitsune battling the Taira ghost samurai.

the dead Taira samurai, rising from their watery graves to drag his ship down.

One warrior spirit broke from the waves and boarded Yoshitsune's boat. It was the fearsome Taira commander Tomomori, who had killed himself, coming for his revenge. Yoshitsune drew his sword, but Benkei realized there was no way his master could win. How could he kill a dead man?

Benkei went to the front of the ship and began praying for the gods to save them. He prayed so strongly and earnestly that he was able to dispel the angry ghosts. They safely reached the far shore. While they survived the attack, neither of them lived much longer. Yoritomo's supporters found them a few years later. Benkei held off their attack, even after having been shot by a dozen arrows, allowing Yoshitsune the noble death, per samurai tradition, of ending his own life.

However, even after Yoshitsune's death, the spirits of the samurai were still not at rest. In his ghost story collection *Kwaidan*, Lafcadio Hearn wrote, "On dark nights thousands of ghostly fires hover about the beach, or flit above the waves—pale lights which the fishermen call Oni-bi, or demon-fires; and, whenever the winds are up, a sound of great shouting comes from that sea, like a clamor of battle." These vengeful spirits were known to try to sink ships and drown swimmers. They also appeared when they were least expected.

One such instance occurred in Akamaséki. In the temple lived a blind man named Hôïchi, who was talented at playing the biwa, a stringed instrument. His most famous song was a retelling of the battle of Dan-no-ura and the terrible death of the Heike clan.

An example of a biwa player, from Shibata Suiha.

On a summer night when the priest was away, Hôïchi was sitting outside on the temple balcony practicing his biwa when he heard an unfamiliar voice call his name. A samurai had come to summon Hôïchi to play for his master, who was very powerful. Afraid to say no, the blind singer followed the man to what he assumed was his master's huge apartment, where he could hear that a large crowd had gathered.

"Then Hôïchi lifted up his voice," Hearn wrote, "and chanted the chant of the fight on the bitter sea—wonderfully making his biwa to sound like the straining of oars and the rushing of ships, the whirr and the hissing of arrows, the shouting and trampling of men, the crashing of steel upon helmets, the plunging of slain in the flood." The crowd was appreciative, and he was asked to come back the next night. However, he was told not to let anyone know where he was going.

The following night, Hôïchi went again, except this time the temple's priest realized he was gone and grew concerned for his blind friend, so he had him followed. Hôïchi walked so fast that the men lost him. They searched the streets in the rainy darkness until they heard the frantic notes of his biwa. They followed the sound to a cemetery.

There was Hôïchi, playing in the rain in front of the gravestone of the long-dead Heike ruler Antoku, and "behind him, and about him, and everywhere above the tombs, the fires of the dead were burning, like candles." He had been bewitched by the demon Oni-bi. This frightened

In Japanese folklore, Oni-bi are angry spirits that have become fire and are seen as floating blue lights. Known as "demon fire," these balls of light are thought to be able to draw the life force out of people, in some cases killing them.

the priest, who—once they returned to the temple—told Hôïchi, "You have put yourself in their power. If you obey them again, after what has already occurred, they will tear you in pieces."

The only way to save Hôïchi was to write holy text on every inch of his body to make him invisible to the spirit. The priest and his assistants worked quickly, covering him with writing before the next nightfall. Then the priest instructed Hôïchi to sit outside on the balcony with his biwa and wait for the spirit. When it came, he was not to respond. If he moved or made a noise, he would be seen and ripped apart by the ghosts.

Hôïchi did as he was told and soon heard his name being called. He did not respond. The spirit couldn't seem to see him. It called his name again and walked around the balcony, stopping close to him.

"Here is the biwa; but of the biwa-player I see—only two ears," said the spirit. "So that explains why he did not answer: he had no mouth to answer with—there is nothing left of him but his ears ... Now to my lord those ears I will take—in proof that the august commands have been obeyed, so far as was possible."

The samurai spirit viciously tore Hôïchi's ears off his head. Hôïchi did not cry out, even though the pain was awful.

The next morning the priest found Hôïchi still sitting on the patio, alive, but with blood oozing from where his ears had been. It seemed that one of the assistants had failed to write the holy text on the poor man's ears.

In the hills above the fishing village of Kotsubo are the tombs of several samurai killed in battle. Locals have seen their spirits perched on a nearby cliff, staring out at the water. In 2015, a Canadian man took a photo of his daughter at the site. Behind her you can see the dark shadow of samurai legs, but no body.

2

TAKE NO PRISONERS

The 1746 Battle of Culloden began as a struggle over who had the right to rule England, Ireland, and Scotland. The rebel group called the Jacobites believed that Charles Stuart, the king's second cousin once removed, had a better claim to the throne than King George II. The battle ended with government troops led by the Duke of Cumberland chasing Charles's fleeing Jacobite soldiers across the Scottish moor. Their orders were to give no quarter, which meant no prisoners would be taken. Instead, every enemy soldier who was caught would be killed.

One government soldier said that what followed was "general carnage. The moor was covered with blood; and our men, what with killing the enemy, dabbling their feet in the blood and splashing it about one another, looked like so many butchers." Another soldier recalled they "could hardly march for dead bodies" covering the ground. For days after the battle, Cumberland's troops slaughtered every enemy soldier they could find, including the wounded who lay on the battlefield. More than 1,200 Jacobites were viciously killed, many buried in piles where they died.

Perhaps that's why on the April 16 anniversary of that terrible bloodbath, ghosts of the fallen soldiers are said to rise and fight once more. The clash of swords and the cries of the wounded are heard echoing over the moors throughout the night.

An Incident at the Rebellion of 1745 was painted soon after the Battle of Culloden, showing Jacobite warriors in tartan plaid fighting government troops.

Prince Charles's grandfather, James, had ruled the countries of England, Ireland, and Scotland from 1685 to 1688 before being overthrown and exiled to Italy. When Charles returned to Scotland in 1745, many people there felt he should be their ruler instead of the current king, George II. Bonnie Prince Charles, as he was known, was able to gather six thousand soldiers, many of them Highlanders from northern Scotland. Known as Jacobites, they began to march against King George's government troops.

The government troops were led by King George's son William, known as the Duke of Cumberland. The

Jacobites met them in a few battles as they made their way into England and won. However, the Jacobites ran low on supplies and decided to retreat back to the Scottish highlands, with the duke's government troops in pursuit.

This portrait of Bonnie Prince Charles, painted while he was in Scotland, was rediscovered after hanging for 250 years in an earl's house.

Before the Battle of Culloden, the highlands of Scotland were ruled by clans, which were groups of people often descended from a common ancestor. Each clan tended to live in a set area, wore a specific tartan plaid, and often had castles. Many clans fought for Prince Charles's Jacobite army, including the McDonalds, Frasers, Chattans, Boyds, and Hays. Their tartan-covered, blood-soaked ghosts have been seen dying on the battlefield.

Bonnie Prince Charles prepared to battle the government troops near Inverness on the Culloden moors, which are open fields. At that time, the government troops, stationed twelve miles away in Nairn, were celebrating Cumberland's birthday.

Charles thought that night would be an ideal time for a surprise attack. The government troops would be distracted and drunk from the birthday celebrations. He sent nearly three thousand of his Jacobite troops. They struggled for miles through the pitch-black woods, trying to get in position to attack. After stumbling around in the dark, they finally realized they couldn't get close enough to Cumberland's camp before dawn. They gave up and went

Centuries later, a woman who lived near Culloden came to the battlefield's visitor center, asking to see the route Charles's troops had taken the night of their failed attack. When she was shown where they traveled on a map, she exclaimed that she knew the route—they had gone right by her house. Several times over the years she had awoken at night to the sound of troops marching but had never seen anything out her window. They were the ghosts of Charles's army!

back to their own camp. Then, when they returned to Culloden, they were forced to begin the battle against the government troops without having slept or eaten.

On April 16, 1746, both sides set up for battle on the icy, wet fields. The British government had approximately 7,800 well-trained, well-fed, well-equipped troops against about 5,250 Jacobites, who were hungry and tired from their failed ambush but still fierce fighters at close range. The Scottish were known for their Highland charge, a terrifying attack with a broadsword and shield.

Cumberland's government troops loaded their cannon

with grapeshot, which was a bag full of small iron balls. Cumberland held his troops back and shot down Charles's attacking lines with rounds of grapeshot across the flat moors. He had also trained his men to defeat the Highland charge using bayonets, which allowed them to get around the Scots' shields. Jacobite Donald Mackay of Acmonie recalled in later years, "The morning was cold and stormy as we stood on the battlefield, snow and rain blowing against us. Before long we saw the red soldiers, in battle formation, in front of us . . . the battle began and the pellets came at us like hail-stones. The big guns were thundering and causing frightful break up among us, but we ran forward and—oh dear!, oh dear!—what cutting and slicing there was and many brave deeds performed."

A British government soldier wrote, "The battle was now entirely fought between swords and bayonets. Our soldiers, by a new practice of using the latter, became much too hard for the swords; and the rebels, as they pushed forward, fell on certain death. Ours at least killed ten to their one in this kind of fighting, besides what fell by the musketry and cannon."

The wet ground made it difficult to retreat when the battle became a bloody massacre. James Johnstone, a Jacobite officer, later wrote that he turned to flee, "but having charged on foot and in my boots, I was so overcome by the marshy ground, the water of which reached to the middle of my legs, that instead of running, I could barely walk." Many Jacobites died trying to escape.

After less than an hour, the main battle was over. Fewer than fifty of Cumberland's troops were killed, while more than a thousand of the Jacobites lay scattered over the moor. Mackay wrote, "The dead lay on all sides and the cries of pain of the wounded rang in our ears. You could see a riderless horse running and jumping as if mad."

Cumberland's troops on horseback pursued the fleeing, defeated Jacobite soldiers, cutting them down on the road. One government soldier later wrote, "'Tis said, that hundreds of the rebels, who have died of their wounds, and of hunger, have been found in the hills at twelve, fourteen, or twenty miles distance from the field of battle; and that their misery is inexpressible." Government soldiers found one group of Jacobite soldiers hiding in a cottage. They locked them in a nearby barn and set it on fire, killing them all. Many of the dead were buried in giant mounds that still dot the battlefield.

On the anniversary of this battle, the last fought on British soil, ghostly sounds of swords clashing and men groaning in pain have been heard by visitors at Culloden. But what isn't heard on these terrible nights is the sound of birdsong. Supposedly, the place is so haunted that birds won't even sing there.

People have also claimed to see a tall Highlander in a tartan kilt walking shell-shocked over the former battlefield. If you manage to get close before he disappears, you can hear him sadly muttering "defeated . . . defeated . . . defeated."

Simon Fraser of Lovat supported the rebel Prince Charles in the rebellion. After the Battle of Culloden, he escaped to an island in Loch Morar. Fraser was eventually found there hiding in the trunk of a tree. He was imprisoned at the dreaded Tower of London, where on April 9, 1747, he became the last person to be beheaded in Britain. His heavy, red-faced ghost has since been seen haunting Loch Morar.

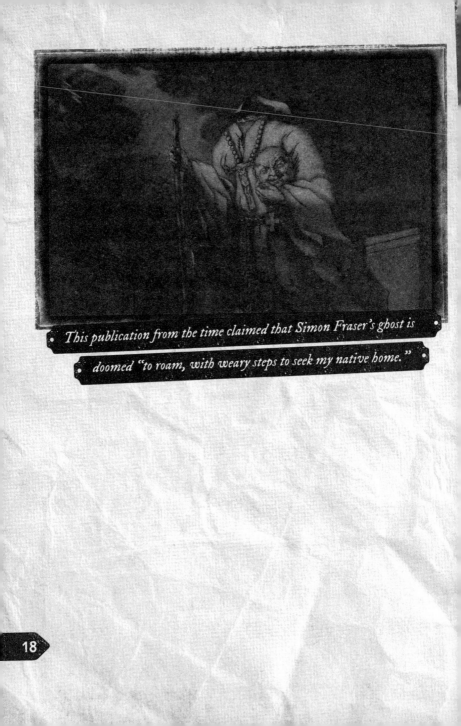

This publication from the time claimed that Simon Fraser's ghost is doomed "to roam, with weary steps to seek my native home."

3

HEADLESS HORSEMAN

Dr. Anthony Baugh's family has lived near present-day Malvern, Pennsylvania, since 1743. His ancestors survived the American Revolution, including the September 21, 1777, battle at the nearby General Paoli Tavern. British troops had surprised Brigadier General Anthony Wayne's sleeping division near the tavern, cutting them to ribbons in a bloody massacre. A Hessian soldier who fought for the British later wrote of that awful night, "We killed three hundred of the rebels with the bayonet. I stuck them myself like so many pigs, one after the other, until the blood ran out of the touch hole of my musket."

Dr. Baugh, described by the *Chester Times* as a "hard-headed practitioner and man of science," knew the town's history well. So when he said he saw a headless ghost in 1932 on the anniversary of the Paoli Massacre, the townsfolk believed him.

The *Times* reported the encounter: "The ghost rode in Paoli last night . . . clad in the blue and buff of the Continental Army." In an interview with the paper, Dr. Baugh said, "the ghostly rider, mounted on a gray horse, rode north on Darby Road from a point about 500 yards out of Lancaster Pike." He had seen the same ghost the year before; so have many others before and since for more than a century. Who was this restless spirit, and where was the headless horseman headed?

☠ ☠ ☠

In September 1777, American commander George Washington ordered Brigadier General Anthony Wayne's Continental Army troops to harass the British troops and attempt to capture their supplies. Wayne had his 1,500 men camp in Paoli, about four miles from the British. He assumed that the British had no idea he was so close. He was dead wrong.

British general Charles Grey quickly learned of the whereabouts of the Continental Army's camp. He came up with a plan for a surprise attack at night. The entire attack would be carried out with bayonets and swords. He had his troops remove the flints from their muskets so the guns

The American Revolutionary War (1775–83) was fought between England and its American colonies, who wanted their independence. The colonists began protesting against taxes imposed by the British, thinking they shouldn't have to pay them if they didn't have a say in the government. This escalated to the first battle, in 1775. The French aided the colonists, known as the Continental Army, and professional German soldiers, known as Hessians, aided the British Army, also known as the redcoats.

would not fire. This seems like a bad idea until you realize that the sound of gunfire alerts your enemy. Also, in the dark, the shot causes a burst of light, which shows the enemy your position.

The British army crept through the woods at night and swooped in on the sleeping Continental troops around midnight.

Charles Grey had fought against the Jacobites in Scotland and in the Seven Years' War before fighting in the American Revolution.

Colonel Thomas Hartley later wrote, "The Enemy last Night at twelve o'clock attacked ... Our Men just raised from Sleep, moved disorderly—Confusion followed ... The Carnage was very great."

Many soldiers awoke to being brutally stabbed in the dark. "I with my own eyes," wrote Lieutenant Colonel Adam Hubley, "see them, cut and hack some of our poor men to pieces after they had fallen on their hands and scarcely shew the least mercy to any ..."

Caught by total surprise, Wayne and his troops fled in terror. Militia member William Hutchinson wrote about one doomed man, "More than a dozen soldiers had with fixed bayonets formed a cordon round him, and that everyone of them in sport had indulged their brutal ferocity by stabbing him in different parts of his body and limbs," and that a physician who examined that soldier found "46 distinct bayonet wounds." The British were thought to have killed some who surrendered as well. In all, 71 soldiers were taken prisoner, 53 killed, and 150 wounded.

Some blamed the American commander, Anthony Wayne, for the massacre of his men. The furious Wayne insisted the matter be brought to court. He was ultimately found not guilty, but Wayne learned from that battle. He used the same strategy of attacking at night with bayonets in a later battle at Stony Point against the British. The

This painting, *A Dreadful Scene of Havock, was painted by request of one of the British soldiers who participated in the attack.*

rallying cry "Remember Paoli" rang out as they stormed the fort.

But who is the spirit of the headless soldier that silently gallops down Darby Road? Stories of his ride have been told for more than a century.

Legend has it that the soldier was one of Wayne's troops, a local man. Because he lived close by, he was able to visit home often. One night when he was sleeping at home, he woke from a nightmare that his fellow troops were being slaughtered. Ignoring the protests of his wife, he got dressed and rode his horse back to camp. There he found

23

In June 1778, Captain Henry Fauntleroy was spending his twenty-second birthday at the Battle of Monmouth. Exhausted, he paused to rest in the Old Tennent Churchyard. Suddenly, a cannonball flew straight at him, shattering his leg and the gravestone nearby. His fellow soldiers carried him into the church and laid him on a pew, where he died. Visitors today can still see the stain of his blood on the pew, which can't be washed away. His ghost has also been seen staring out the church window at night.

Captain Fauntleroy's grave at the Old Tennent Churchyard.

a bloodbath. Before he could get away, he was beheaded by British troops.

On every anniversary of the massacre, this poor soldier is doomed to repeat the fateful ride to his death. Some have said that if the rider stops and hands you his cut-off head, you will die before the end of the year.

GENERAL "MAD ANTHONY" WAYNE'S RESTLESS GHOST

4

PENNSYLVANIA, DECEMBER 3, 1796

After the Revolutionary War, white American settlers spread to lands north of the Ohio River formerly held by the British. This led to brutal and violent conflicts between the settlers and the Native Americans who had always lived there and considered the land theirs. President George Washington had to find a way to defeat them.

One of Washington's challenges was that he didn't have an army. After the Revolutionary War, the army had been disbanded. So he created the First American Regiment under the leadership of General Josiah Harmar. Harmar trained the men in the European style of combat, which had troops lining up on a battlefield.

In October 1790, Harmar's troops marched out in a

line to confront the Miami, Shawnee, and Potawatomi tribes, led by Miami chief Little Turtle. They were cut down at every turn. They floundered fighting in the dense woods that the tribes used to their advantage. It was such a slaughter that Native Americans called the final conflict against Harmar the "Battle of the Pumpkin Field" because the fields full of bloody heads from dead US soldiers reminded them of pumpkins.

Chief Little Turtle, considered one of the best Native American leaders, won a number of major victories against US forces.

The second general appointed by Washington, Arthur St. Clair, fared even worse than Harmar. In November 1791, the Native American forces killed more than six hundred troops, along with around two hundred camp followers, including women and children. It would prove to be the most people killed in any battle between the United States and Native Americans in history. St. Clair survived the massacre and was promptly asked to resign.

That's when Washington turned to a man known for

getting things done—Major General "Mad Anthony" Wayne, who had survived the Paoli massacre and helped lead the Continental Army to victory in the Revolutionary War.

☠ ☠ ☠

Why did Washington ask Wayne to come out of retirement to fight the Native Americans? He knew Wayne could inspire, train, and terrify troops into winning battles. During the Revolutionary War, Washington had commended him for "good conduct and bravery" for his

At the end of the American Revolutionary War, the British agreed to give up control of the areas known as the Ohio Country and Illinois Country. However, these lands were home to a number of Indigenous American peoples, as well as British trading forts. Since the British had been supported by the Native Americans during the revolution, they continued to supply them with guns. Bloody conflicts between the Native Americans and white settlers and troops were known as the Northwest Indian War.

troops' successes at the battles of Brandywine, Monmouth, and Germantown.

In July 1779, Washington had considered attacking Stony Point, a well-defended fort held by the British. Wayne replied, "Issue the order, and I'll storm hell!" And he did.

Wayne led a group of elite troops in a well-planned nighttime bayonet attack. Although he was shot in the head during the attack, he said, "Forward, my brave fellows, forward! Carry me into the fort. If I am to die, I want to die at the head of the column!" He survived and took the fort and the British troops prisoner. He wrote to Washington, "The fort and garrison, with Colonel Johnston, are ours. Our officers and men behaved like men who are determined to be free." For his bravery, Wayne received one of the few medals awarded during the Revolutionary War.

Though Wayne was calm in battle, his nickname, "Mad Anthony," endured for a number of reasons. During the Revolutionary War, troops often threatened to mutiny because of a lack of supplies, food, or payment. Wayne had to quash a number of these rebellions, in some cases even executing their leaders, which he did in front of all his troops so they knew not to mutiny again.

Beyond his leadership skills, Wayne was also quite a

On July 16, 1780, the Iroquois, who were fighting in the Revolutionary War on behalf of the British, surprised a group of rangers led by Captain William Phillips in an abandoned home. The rangers were outnumbered but fought bravely until the house was set on fire, which forced their surrender. Once captured, they were tied to nearby trees by the Iroquois, tortured, and then killed. Their bodies were later buried in a mass grave. The rangers' restless spirits are said to appear on the anniversary of the battle, including one shadowy figure who watches over the grave each year.

character. He liked fine food and dress and made sure his troops were as well outfitted as possible. Wayne was also known for his exceptionally foul language—which is saying something, since soldiers were known for their swearing.

After the British surrender in Yorktown at the end of the Revolutionary War, Wayne's troops were sent south

Wayne was known as a general who led from the front lines, which meant he was often first into battle.

to fight the Native Americans supported by the British in Georgia. Once he subdued them, he left the army in 1783.

Then, in 1792, Wayne came out of retirement. He was appointed by President George Washington to command the new Legion Army. While the US government attempted to negotiate peace with the Native Americans, Wayne trained his soldiers to fight them. For two years, he drilled his troops, even employing war games that simulated a Native American attack.

Throughout this time, Wayne suffered from malaria

and painful bouts of gout, a disease that comes on suddenly and makes it feel like your joints are on fire. However, he remained a tough leader. Major William Eaton later wrote, "I have seen him, in the most severe night of the winter of 1794, sleep on the ground, like his fellow-soldiers, and walk around the camp at four in the morning, with the vigilance of a sentinel."

On August 20, 1794, Wayne's three thousand troops defeated the Native American alliance in what was called the Battle of Fallen Timbers. They continued their march, burning the Native people's crops and destroying villages along the way. This show of strength led to the Treaty of Greenville, in which tribes gave up significant lands in Ohio to white American settlers.

In December 1796, Wayne was in Fort Presque Isle, Pennsylvania, when his gout became terrible. Captain Henry DeButts wrote, "It by turns affected his feet, knees and hands, with considerable inflammation and a great degree of pain . . . on the morning of the 3d inst. [December 3, 1796], it appeared that the gout had taken possession of his stomach, where it remained with unconquerable obstinacy and extreme torture, until it put a period to his existence." Upon his death, Wayne was dressed in his finest uniform and buried near the fort's flag.

In 1809, Wayne's family decided to move his remains

Native American warriors set up their defenses behind a line of trees that had been knocked down by a tornado. They thought it might hide them and stop Wayne's cavalry, but in the Battle of Fallen Timbers, it did not help as much as they had hoped.

to the family cemetery in southern Pennsylvania. They paid Dr. J. C. Wallace to dig up the body and get it ready for travel. Wallace was surprised to find that, even though twelve years had passed, the general's corpse had held up well. Since a rotting body would not travel well for hundreds of miles in a wagon, Wallace was then tasked with boiling the flesh off the body. He boxed the clean bones for travel and reburied the other remains, including the pot, in Presque Isle. Wayne's son took the bones back to the family's plot in Radnor. Some say the wagon bounced so much that a few of the general's bones were lost along the way.

Since his body rests in two places, Wayne's spirit is said to thunder along the roads between. On his birthday of January 1, his ghost, astride his horse Nancy, is seen searching for his lost bones.

How many Revolutionary War generals are fictional ancestors to a superhero? Just Anthony Wayne, who in the DC Comics universe is related to Bruce Wayne, also known as Batman. When Bill Finger helped create the character, he used the general as an inspiration for Bruce Wayne's name. Later comic book writers and artists explored the history between them, including a time-travel story where Anthony Wayne and Bruce Wayne meet.

5

BLOWN TO BITS

Jarvis Hanks was fourteen years old when he joined the American Army as a drummer boy, which broke his mother's heart. For a $20 signing bonus and 160 acres when discharged, Hanks agreed to stay in the army for the entire War of 1812. The recruiter promised his grieving mother that Hanks would not be on the front lines. The recruiter lied.

Hanks was stationed at Fort Erie when the British, led by Lieutenant Colonel William Drummond, attacked on August 15, 1814. Hanks later wrote in his memoirs, "The night was rainy and extremely dark; and as anticipated, the attack commenced at two in the morning. The enemy came with bayonets, scaling ladders, hand grenades and [bundles of sticks]. Every one of them was supplied with an extra half-pint of rum for the strengthening and whetting up his courage; to make him fierce and brave in the attack and reckless of danger to himself."

The British succeeded in using ladders to reach the top of the bastion, which stuck out from the top of the wall of the fort. They began turning the gun they captured toward the Americans when, as Hanks remembered, "an awful explosion occurred which blew up the bastion; sent, in a moment, near two hundred of our enemies into eternity; caused the remainder to retreat with terror to their camp; and closed the contest for the present."

After the sun had risen, Hanks went out to see the carnage. He "counted 196 bodies lying in the ditch and about the fort; most of them dead; some dying. Their faces and hands were burned black, many of them were horribly mutilated. Here and there were legs, arms and heads lying in confusion, separated by the concussion from the trunks to which they had long been attached. One trunk I observed, deprived of all its limbs and head." The Americans roughly buried all the British dead in a large ditch near the fort.

These were just a few of the many who perished during the Siege of Fort Erie. Today, it is considered one of the most haunted places in Canada. The sound of long-ago gunfire is common, and spirits of soldiers have been seen in the area, among other shadowy figures.

Fort Erie is located on the Niagara River, across from Buffalo, New York.

The War of 1812 (1812–15) was fought among the United States, the United Kingdom, and their Canadian and Native American allies. It had a number of causes, including the British restricting American trade and kidnapping American sailors, and the United States' desire for more territory.

The War of 1812 had been ongoing for two years along the Canadian border. The Americans settled into Fort Erie, located on the Niagara River across from Buffalo, New York. About 2,200 soldiers, under the command of Brigadier General Edmund Pendleton Gaines, defended the well-fortified camp, which backed up to the river.

In August 1814, British lieutenant general Sir Gordon Drummond (William's uncle) and his 3,000 men were tasked with taking the fort from the Americans, which he wrote would be a "great hazard," considering "the strength of the enemy's position and the number of men and guns by which it is defended." His plan was a siege, which meant surrounding the fort and cutting off its supplies. Once

Before a fort was built on this land, it was a sacred burial ground for approximately 400 Algonquin and Iroquois people. Their spirits have been spotted as a blue-green mist, which is thought to be a good omen. They are most often seen in the winter, when the colorful mist stands out against the snow.

in position, his troops would bombard the fort until the Americans surrendered.

Unfortunately for General Drummond, his engineer didn't have experience building fieldwork, the platforms from which British artillery would bomb the fort. They spent days constructing it, all while being shot at by the Americans, only to find that it was positioned too far away. Their guns could barely reach the fort. But a lucky shot on August 14 hit a chest of ammunition, causing a massive explosion.

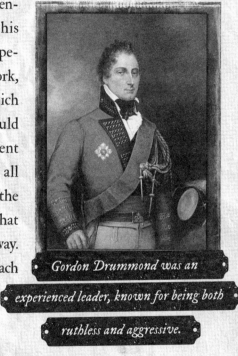

Gordon Drummond was an experienced leader, known for being both ruthless and aggressive.

Drummond assumed that the explosion had weakened the American forces, so he planned a surprise attack that night. He assumed wrong—few soldiers had actually been killed. Worse, a deserter from the British Army had told the Americans of Drummond's plan, so it was no longer a surprise.

Three columns of British soldiers made their way in darkness through the woods and across the icy river. Their guns were disabled, so there was no chance the sound of gunfire would alert the Americans. But as they neared the fort, a hail of American gunfire lit up the night, killing numerous British soldiers. Two columns were forced to withdraw.

However, the column under Colonel Drummond managed to scale the walls of the fort under heavy fire. As Jarvis Hanks had described, when they finally succeeded in reaching the top of the wall, it exploded. Lieutenant David Douglass had a haunting memory of the moment: "Every sound was hushed by the sense of an unnatural tremor beneath our feet like the first heave of an earthquake. Almost at the same instant the center of the bastion blew up with a terrific explosion and a jet of flame mingled with fragments of timber, earth, stone, and bodies of men rose to the height of one or two hundred feet in the air and fell in a shower of ruins to a great distance all around."

Colonel John Le Couteur wrote to his brother that after being blown up and retreating to the British lines, "in a fit of sorrow I threw my sabre down exclaiming, 'This is a disgraceful day for Old England!' Col. M—, who heard me, said, 'For shame, Mr. Le Couteur! The men are sufficiently discouraged by defeat.' Col. Pearson said, 'Don't blame him. It is the high feeling of a young soldier.' To my surprise the Commander-in-chief, Sir Gordon

Drummond, had heard all this as he was close behind
and he asked me, 'Where is Col. Scott?' 'Oh! Sir! He is
killed, just being brought in by his men.' 'Where is Col.
Drummond?' 'Alas! Sir! He is killed too. Bayonetted.' And
I burst into tears at the loss of my beloved commander
and three parts of my men."

While it was a victory for the Americans, the siege
continued for another month. Men on both sides were
killed daily. Jarvis Hanks wrote, "As there were no regu-
lar barbers attached to the army, the soldiers used to shave
themselves, and each other. One morning several were

41

shaving in succession, near a parapet [wall]. Sergeant Wait sat down facing the enemy, and Corporal Reed began to perform the operation of removing the beard from his face, when a cannon ball took the Corporal's right hand, and the Sergeant's head; throwing blood, brains, hair, fragments of flesh and bones, upon a tent near them, and upon the clothing of several spectators of the horrible scene." Reed's arms were amputated and he was thought to have died soon after. The headless Wait was immediately buried near where he died.

On September 17, in heavy rains, the Americans attacked. They disabled British cannon and blew up ammunition. Four days later, the British retreated across the river. After 791 were killed and wounded for the British and nearly as many for the Americans, the siege was finally over. In November, preparing for the coming winter, the Americans blew up the fort and abandoned it.

However, the ruins have not been abandoned by the spirits of the many men who lost their lives there. In the years following the battle, townspeople claimed to see two ghosts along the banks of the Niagara River. One had no hands and the other had no head. Later, when Jarvis Hanks's memoir came to light, it became obvious who they were—Sergeant Wait and Corporal Reed. In 1987, their bodies were found buried near the old fort. They were reburied with honors, and the hauntings have ceased.

The ghost of a woman has also been seen in an area that used to be a mess hall for the soldiers. While no record exists of a woman dying during the siege, women did work in that area. Her spirit was even captured in a recent photograph taken of the room.

Fort George is about thirty miles north of Fort Erie on Lake Ontario. During the War of 1812, it was also the site of brutal battles and bloody deaths. A number of spirits have been seen lurking about, opening and closing doors. The most well-known is the playful ghost of a little girl, Sarah Ann Tracey, the daughter of a military man, who died at age seven in 1840. She is said to play peekaboo and tug visitors' coats and run away.

6

VICTORY OR DEATH!

David "Davy" Crockett was already famous when he joined Texas's fight for independence from Mexico in 1836. A frontiersman who knew how to tell a great story, Crockett had led an adventurous life. He ran away from home at age thirteen and traveled the country, performing odd jobs. An expert marksman, he claimed to have killed 105 bears in one seven-month period. He was a soldier and scout before running for Congress in 1827 and winning. His popular stories on the campaign trail led him to write an auto-biography, which became a national bestseller. After losing a Congressional race in 1835, Crockett told a crowd, "I told the people of my District, that, if they saw fit to re-elect me, I would serve them as faithfully as I had done, but, if not, they might go to hell, and I would go to Texas."

Crockett arrived in the Mexican province of Texas in February 1836, leading a group of fourteen men known as the Tennessee Mountain Rifles. His help was welcomed in the town of San Antonio de Béxar, which was under the control of a small band of Texas rebels led by James Bowie

Davy Crockett in his signature buckskin.

and William Barret Travis. When Mexican general Santa Anna attacked the town with thousands of troops on February 23, Crockett and fewer than two hundred men moved the fight to a fortresslike former church, which Spanish troops formerly stationed there had named the Alamo. For thirteen days, they withstood the artillery of the Mexican troops. In a letter that was smuggled out on February 25, William Travis wrote, "The Hon. David Crockett was seen at all points, animating the men to do their duty."

When Santa Anna's forces finally overwhelmed the Alamo on March 6, the general ordered his troops to kill every rebel. While there were conflicting reports about how Crockett died, a diary of Santa Anna's lieutenant colonel José Enrique de la Peña claims that "some seven men had survived the general carnage and, under the protection of General Castrillón, they were brought before Santa Anna. Among them . . . was the naturalist David Crockett, well known in North America for his unusual adventures." Santa Anna ordered their immediate execution. De la Peña wrote that his soldiers, "with swords in hand, fell upon these unfortunate, defenseless men just as a tiger leaps upon his prey. Though tortured before they were killed, these unfortunates died without complaining and without humiliating themselves before their torturers."

Just days after the slaughter of the Texas troops, visitors to the Alamo began to report ghost sightings. Since that battle, many people have claimed to see the spirit of Crockett, wearing his distinctive racoon-skin cap and carrying his flintlock rifle, standing at attention outside the chapel. As Crockett wrote to his family when he arrived in Texas, "Do not be uneasy about me. I am among friends." It appears his spirit has chosen to stay.

💀 💀 💀

One reason the phrase "Remember the Alamo" and the small fort have become so famous are the letters written by

William Barret Travis during the thirteen-day siege. The

In 1821, Mexico, which included Texas, declared independence from Spain. Mexico allowed Americans to settle in Texas, and soon they greatly outnumbered the Mexican residents. Tensions between the Texans and the Mexican government grew, culminating in the Texas Revolution. The Republic of Texas declared their independence from Mexico on March 2, 1836, just days before the Battle of the Alamo. The republic became a part of the United States in 1845.

most famous reads: "FELLOW-CITIZENS AND COMPATRIOTS: I am besieged by a thousand or more of the Mexicans under Santa Anna. I have sustained a continued bombardment for twenty-four hours, and have not lost a man. The enemy have demanded a surrender at discretion . . . I have answered the summons with a cannon-shot, and our flag still waves proudly from the walls. I shall never surrender or retreat . . . Victory or Death!"

Santa Anna assured the rebels that they would all be

Not many images exist of William Travis. This one was created after his death, and the artist had never seen nor met Travis.

killed. Travis wrote, "A blood red banner waves from the church of Bexar, and in the camp above us, in token that the war is one of vengeance against rebels; they have declared us as such; demanded, that we should surrender at discretion, or that this garrison should be put to the sword. Their threats have had no influence on me or my men, but to make all fight with desperation, and that high souled courage which characterizes the patriot, who is willing to die in defense of his country's liberty and his own honor."

And die they did. Waves of Mexican troops attacked the fort in the dark predawn hours of March 6, fighting their way up the Alamo's thick walls. Travis was quickly killed by a gunshot to the head. De la Peña described the chaotic scene: "The sharp retort of the rifles, the whistling of bullets, the groans of the wounded, the cursing of the men, the sighs and anguished cries of the dying, the inordinate shouts of the attackers, who climbed vigorously, bewildered all."

Eight-year-old Enrique Esparza's father was one of the Texan soldiers. Enrique was hiding in the chapel with him when, he later recalled, "there was a terrible din. Cannon boomed. Their shot crashed through the doors and windows and the breeches in the walls. Then men rushed in on us. They swarmed among us and over us ... And so my father died fighting. He struck down one of his foes as he fell in the heap of the slain." After Crockett and the six other remaining rebels were caught and executed, most of the approximately two hundred Texans killed were piled up and burned. An estimated six hundred Mexican soldiers died, making it a costly battle for Santa Anna.

News of the slaughter at the Alamo reached the American newspapers. Inspired by the rebels' heroic struggle, hundreds of men rushed to join the Texas independence movement. At the end of April, the Texans defeated Santa Anna at the Battle of San Jacinto, many yelling "Remember the Alamo!" as they rushed into the fray.

Throughout its history, the Alamo has been plagued by ghosts. In February 1894, the *San Antonio Express News* wrote, "The Alamo is again in the center of interest to quite a number of curious people who have been attracted by the

49

After the battle, General Juan José de Andrade and his troops were ordered by Santa Anna to destroy the Alamo. As they approached the building, six fiery spirits were said to have appeared, yelling "Do not touch these walls!" Some say that is why the building is still standing.

rumors of the manifestations of alleged ghosts who are said to be holding bivouac [camp] around that place so sacred to the memory of Texas' historic dead. There is nothing new about the stories told. There is the same measured tread of the ghostly sentry as he crosses the south side of the roof from east to west; the same tale of buried treasure."

At one point, the city of San Antonio considered using the Alamo as a jail. However, there were so many incidents of terrifying shadows and unexplained noises that the city council decided it would be "cruel and unusual punishment" to have prisoners locked up there. The building was later turned into a museum.

Museum staff and visitors have reported seeing numerous ghosts. Vincent Phillip, former chief of the Alamo Rangers, has described seeing an Alamo defender wearing a white shirt, light brown pants, a long brown coat, and high black boots. The spirit appears to be fleeing from

The Alamo at night can be creepy, with many people claiming to have seen ghosts.

the Long Barracks with a frantic look on his face. He runs a few steps and then disappears into thin air.

The most unexplainable ghost that appears at the Alamo is a small blond boy who has appeared throughout the fort, especially in windows on the higher floors. Some children have said he has spoken with them. Some believe the spirit is searching for a loved one who died in the battle.

7
A HARVEST OF DEATH

On July 1, 1863, the Confederate soldiers of Alfred Iverson's North Carolina Brigade advanced across an open farmland battlefield in Gettysburg, Pennsylvania. Normally some soldiers, called skirmishers, would have been sent ahead to scout for enemy troops. None were sent on that hot day. Iverson's men would pay the price.

Rising from a low stone wall, enemy Union soldiers released a deafening volley of gunfire. Hundreds of Confederates were cut down dead. A soldier later wrote that the North Carolina Brigade had died so quickly that after the slaughter they were "laying dead in a line, perfectly dressed . . . Three had fallen to the front, the rest had fallen backward, yet the feet of all of these men were in a perfectly straight line." Out of the 1,470 troops in the brigade, more than 500 were killed and wounded and 300 were missing. Some say this was the most deadly minute of the Civil War.

When the Union forces won the bloody battle two days later, they gathered their fallen troops for burial. However, the Confederate dead were quickly buried where they fell in shallow graves that became known as "Iverson's Pits." Plants grew in a straight green line over their graves, nourished on the bodies of the North Carolina Brigade.

After the battle, farmworkers avoided that area after nightfall. Stories began circulating of ghostly moans and odd lights coming from the pits. In more recent years, otherworldly voices have been recorded at the site. These are just some of the many ghost sightings on this blood-soaked battlefield.

The American Civil War began in 1861 when the Northern and Southern states fought each other over whether or not slavery should be abolished. The Union Army of the North defeated the Southern Confederate Army in 1865, after the death of more than 620,000 men.

The Battle of Gettysburg was the death-filled turning point of an already horrific Civil War. Confederate leader Robert E. Lee brought his troops into the North, where they clashed with George Meade's Union Army. In three short days, the largest battle ever fought on American soil caused nearly 28,000 casualties for the South and 25,000 for the North.

In a letter to his wife, Calvin A. Haynes of the Union's 125th New York Infantry wrote that, for him, the second

The Union and Confederate armies faced off on either side of a 30-acre cornfield, which over the course of the bloody battle became a killing field.

afternoon was the bloodiest part of the battle: "At 2 p.m. they opened on us . . . with over a 100 cannon. We lay flat on our faces for 2 hours. The air was filled with shell bursting in every direction. The battery that lay in front of us had 55 horses and 80 men killed . . . That night and the next day [the Rebels] retreated leaving their dead and wounded on the field. I went over the field. Such a sight I never wish to see again. Every conceivable wound that can be thought of was there. There was so many wounded that it was impossible to attend to all of them."

After the Union Army won the battle, corpses littered the fields and roads of the small Pennsylvania town, including nearly 3,000 horses. Photographers Timothy

Opened originally in 1815, Cashtown Inn, eight miles west of Gettysburg, was a Confederate Army camp where many wounded soldiers died. It is still used as an inn today, with rooms named for Confederate generals. The spirit of a soldier is said to walk the halls and knock on the door of room 4 in the middle of the night. He appears standing in front of the inn in an 1895 photo taken from across the street.

O'Sullivan and Alexander Gardner took images that showed the American people the terrible result of war. In the caption for one photo, Gardner wrote, "Slowly, over the misty field of Gettysburg . . . came the sunless morn, after the retreat of Lee's broken army. Through the shadowy vapors, it was, indeed, a 'harvest of death' that was presented; hundreds and thousands of torn Union and rebel soldiers . . . strewed the now quiet fighting ground, soaked by the rain, which for two days had drenched the country in its fitful showers."

Without enough people to bury the dead and care for

Photographs like this one, entitled Harvest of Death, *allowed many Americans to see an actual battlefield for the first time.*

the wounded, the townspeople were overwhelmed. One local woman later said, "Wounded men were brought into our houses and laid side-by-side in our halls and rooms. Carpets were so saturated with blood as to be unfit for further use. Walls were bloodstained, as well as books that were used as pillows."

Elsewhere in Gettysburg, Brigadier General William Barksdale led a Confederate brigade into battle, yelling "Advance! Advance! Brave Mississippians, one more charge and the day is ours!" But then, according to a fellow general, "Barksdale, gallantly leading his men in the terrific fight, fell mortally wounded. The last words of that ardent patriot to fall on the ears of one of his countrymen were, 'I am killed. Tell my wife and children I died fighting at my post.'" Barksdale was brought to the nearby farmhouse of the Hummelbaugh family, where in a fever he repeatedly called for water

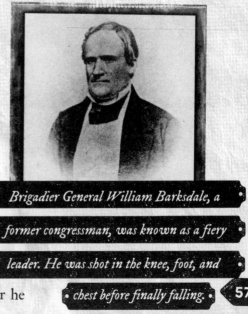

Brigadier General William Barksdale, a former congressman, was known as a fiery leader. He was shot in the knee, foot, and chest before finally falling.

57

before dying. He was buried in the backyard, where his ghostly cries for water can still be heard.

Some say that Barksdale's wife came with his dog to collect his body. The dog immediately went to his grave and began howling. When she began her trip home, he refused to leave his master's grave. The dog was said to have died of dehydration a week later. His howls are heard on summer nights.

James Culbertson was a Confederate soldier from South Carolina. His brother-in-law, H. J. Douvall, was fighting alongside him when Culbertson was shot. Douvall wrote in August to Culbertson's wife, Eliza, about how Culbertson died: "He got shot directly as we went into the fight. He was shot in the leg and through the shoulder. After the fight was over we carried him to a house and me and 3 or 4 men stayed with him all night. He died about twelve O'clock in the night and we buried him the next day. He was put away the best we could do it. The grave had planks in the bottom of it and his oil cloth was put under him and his blanket was put around him, and there was planks put over him to keep the dirt off of him." His ghost is said to haunt the halls of the Gettysburg Hotel, which is situated a few blocks away from the battlefield.

The Union Twentieth Maine Regiment was rushing to Gettysburg when they came to a crossroads. They weren't sure which way to go. According to reports, the ghostly figure of George Washington on a white horse appeared. The figure raised his finger, silently pointing them in the right direction and allowing them to arrive in time for them to stop a Confederate attack. So many soldiers claimed to see Washington's ghost that day that the secretary of war investigated the incident. The regiment's commander, Colonel Joshua Chamberlain, testified, "Who shall say that Washington was not among the number of those who aided the country that he founded?"

8

CUSTER'S DOOMED STAND

• BATTLE OF LITTLE BIGHORN, MONTANA, JUNE 26, 1876 •

Less than an hour into the battle at the Little Bighorn River, it had already turned into a slaughter. George Armstrong Custer and approximately fifty soldiers were surrounded by Native Americans on a high ridge, fighting for their lives.

Custer was originally supposed to be joined by two other army columns to help force the Native Americans out of the Black Hills and onto reservations. But when he encountered a large group of Lakota Sioux and Northern Cheyenne camped along the river, he didn't wait for the other columns.

Afraid that Native scouts would alert the tribes to their

Custer's column of cavalry, artillery, and wagons crossing the plains of the Dakota Territory in 1874.

presence, Custer divided his 700 troops of the Seventh Cavalry and quickly launched a three-pronged attack. This was a huge mistake. Custer believed they were facing around 800 warriors. It was more like 1,800.

Custer and his five companies of 210 men each held off the warriors for a short while. "We chased the soldiers up a long, gradual slope or hill in a direction away from the river and over the ridge where the battle began in good earnest," said Shave Elk, a Sioux warrior.

Some say that's when the Native "suicide boys" attacked. These warriors had decided before the battle that they would keep fighting until they were killed. To prepare, they performed the "Dying Dance" and paraded through the encampment the night before. The Battle of Little Bighorn was their day to die.

As the battle grew hot, a group of more than twenty of these warriors surged unexpectedly up the hill. This forced Custer's men into hand-to-hand combat instead of shooting from a distance. In the chaos, more Native Americans joined in the fight and frightened off the soldiers' horses, taking away their only means of escape.

Many Natives died during the battle and their bodies were taken from the battlefield by their tribes. Later interviews with those who participated in the battle said the suicide boys were among the dead.

More than a hundred years later, Mardell Plainfeather, a park ranger, was working late one night at the former battlefield. She looked up on the bluffs and saw the ghosts of two Native braves. They were sitting on horses, dressed for battle, with feathers in their hair. Had she seen these long-dead warriors?

When Custer divided his troops into three groups on June 25, he gave three companies to Captain Frederick

The Great Sioux War (1876–77) was also known as the Black Hills War because the US government wanted this land, which was owned by the Lakota Sioux and the Northern Cheyenne. Gold was discovered in the Black Hills and settlers from the United States rushed into this area. The government offered to buy the land but the tribes refused, since it was not only sacred to their culture, it was their home. Over a two-year period, a combination of military force and negotiations forced the tribes to move out of the Black Hills and onto reservations.

Benteen to go southwest and three companies to Major Marcus Reno to attack the Native American camp from the south. They charged down the valley and, for a few miles, were chasing Natives who appeared to be running away. But they weren't retreating—they were drawing the troops into a trap. Reno wrote later, "I could not see Custer or any other support, and at the same time the very earth seemed to grow Indians, and they were running toward me in swarms, and from all directions. I saw I must defend

The painter Edgar Paxson spent twenty years interviewing and researching the battle before creating Custer's Last Stand, which includes more than two hundred people.

myself and give up the attack mounted." He had his troops dismount along the edge of the woods for protection and to battle the incoming warriors.

But Reno was losing men in the fierce fighting, including his Native American scout, Bloody Knife, who was shot in the head while Reno was talking to him. They had to move. Reno and his men made a desperate dash through the river to the bluffs on the other side, during which a number of men were killed, including a man named Lieutenant Benjamin H. Hodgson.

Private William Slaper later wrote about seeing Hodgson die: "As I glanced about me, the first thing that engaged my attention was Trumpeter Henry Fisher of M Troop, riding in the river some distance up, with Lieut. Benny Hodgson hanging to one stirrup. Hodgson had been wounded and was on foot in the stream, when Fisher came dashing into the water. Noting Hodgson's helpless condition, he thrust one of his stirrups toward him, which Hodgson grasped and was thus towed across to the opposite bank, under a galling fire from the Indians, who were now riding into the stream, shooting into the ranks of the

Second Lieutenant Benjamin H. Hodgson was a brave soldier admired by his troops and commanders alike. Following the chaos of the battle, his was one of the few bodies recovered and buried on the battlefield. Perhaps this is why his ghost has been seen on the battlefield so often. In 1983, a woman named Christine Hope had been working and living at the battlefield park. She awoke at about 2:00 a.m. one night in early fall to see the ghost of a man with a long mustache sitting at her kitchen table. He stared at her sorrowfully for a moment before disappearing. She later recognized him from photos as Benjamin Hodgson.

This wasn't the first time Hodgson has reached out from beyond the grave. In 1877, Clinton Tebbetts, a close friend of Hodgson's from the US Military Academy at West Point, went to see a noted psychic. The psychic asked Tebbetts to write a question on a piece of paper and roll it up. He wrote a question to the spirit of Hodgson, who had died at Little Bighorn the year before, asking, "Dear Friend. Did Custer's command go into his last fight willingly or not?" The psychic wrote out a response dictated from Hodgson's ghost: "We of course went in willingly for we never deemed defeat possible. We were anxious for combat with the [Indians], and we had it too, but their numbers were too much for us, and we died gallantly."

stampeding troopers, and actually pulling many of them from their horses right there in the river. As Fisher gained the opposite bank, dragging Hodgson at the end of his stirrup, and the latter was trying to struggle up the incline, another shot rang out and Hodgson dropped. I did not see him move again, and suppose he was killed right there."

Captain Benteen's men eventually joined Reno's men on the bluffs. As night fell, Reno had his men prepare for the next day's fight. They dug rifle pits and built barricades out of dead horses, mules, and boxes of hard bread while the Natives sang and performed a war dance in the dark nearby. Reno kept expecting Custer's men to join them, not realizing that they had all already been killed in their stand on the hill.

At daybreak, the roar of gunfire began again. If any part of a soldier was not hidden, it was hit. "We could see, as the day brightened, countless hordes of [Indians] pouring up the valley from the village and scampering over the high points toward the places designated for them by their chiefs, and which entirely surrounded our position," Reno later recalled. "I think we were fighting all the Sioux Nation."

Later that afternoon, the Native Americans set fire to the area beneath the bluff, creating a huge cloud of smoke, which confused Reno and his men. They later realized it was to hide the Native Americans while they packed up their camp because they had learned that another column of the army under General Alfred Terry was due to arrive. Reno wrote, "It was between 6 and 7 p.m. that the village came out from behind the dense clouds of smoke and dust. We had a close and good view of them as they filed away in the direction of the Big Horn Mountains, moving in almost perfect military order."

When Terry's column arrived, Reno learned that Custer and his companies had been wiped out. Their bodies had been stripped and then mutilated by the Native Americans, who believed that the way the body is in death is how the soul remains in the afterlife. When the news hit the papers, there was intense outrage, as Custer had been a well-known Civil War hero. Many criticized Reno for not coming to Custer's aid, but he felt his men would have been slaughtered if they had.

The area where so many died in Black Hills became a memorial. In the years after the battle, local Crow people avoided the area at night. They called the superintendent of the park "ghost herder." The Crow believed that when the superintendent lowered the flag at night, the spirits of the soldiers and warriors rose from their graves and walked among the living. When the flag was raised in the morning, the dead came back to rest . . . until the next night.

Captain Myles Keogh's horse, Comanche.

Captain Myles Keogh was the commander, under Custer, of Company I of the Seventh Cavalry. He was killed when Sioux and Cheyenne warriors overran the ridge. His horse, Comanche, was found wounded but alive after the battle. Comanche was considered one of the few survivors and was nursed back to health.

9

GHOSTS OF THE WESTERN FRONT

Much of World War I was fought in the trenches of the Western Front, a four hundred-mile stretch of battlefields through France to the coast of Belgium. The Allied and Central Power armies dug these long, deep ditches and then fought from the relative safety of underground. Occasionally an army would surge into the open space between the trenches, known as "no-man's-land." More often than not, that surge would get them killed. It was dangerous to recover the dead, so the bodies would often be left lying there.

Millions of soldiers lived for years in the trenches, which filled with mud when it rained and froze to ice when it was cold. Overrun with rats, lice, and fleas, the soldiers were never clean or dry and it was hard to sleep. Artillery would explode nearby, burying soldiers alive in the pits. So many bodies mixed in the bombed earth that hands, heads, and feet would poke out of the ground.

"We are all used to dead bodies or pieces of men, so much so that we are not troubled by the sight of them," wrote one Canadian soldier. "There was a right hand sticking out of the trench in the position of a man trying to shake hands with you, and as the men filed out they would often grip it and say, 'So long, old top, we'll be back again soon.'"

Frank Iriam, a sniper in the First Canadian Division, described how frightening it was to be alongside these

Canadian soldiers examining a skull on Vimy Ridge.

fallen soldiers on the Western Front. "You could feel the pulse of the thousands of dead with their pale hands protruding through the mud here and there and seeming to beckon you," he wrote in his memoir. "You could feel the presence of something not of this earth. Akin to goblins." And Iriam was not the only soldier haunted by their spirits.

Another Canadian soldier wrote to his mother, "One night while carrying bombs, I had occasion to take cover when about twenty yards off I saw you looking towards me as plain as life." Shocked, he crawled toward this vision of his mother. A German shell suddenly exploded where he had previously been. "Had it not been for you, I certainly would have been reported 'missing,'" the soldier wrote. "You'll turn up again, won't you, mother, next time a shell is coming?"

When the British Empire declared war against the Central Powers, Canada entered the war with them. Both armies fought for years without making significant advances. One area that saw a lot of action was Vimy Ridge, a long, high hill in northern France. The Germans had captured it early in the war and built an extensive tunnel system underground. Unsuccessful attempts to recapture the hill in 1914 and 1915 by the British and French led to hundreds of thousands of deaths.

World War I (1914–18) was fought between the Allied Powers (France, Russia, Britain, and later the United States) and the Central Powers (Germany, Austria-Hungary, the Ottoman Empire, and Bulgaria) to determine which would be the dominant power in Europe and parts of the Middle East and Africa.

The Canadians were tasked with making another attempt in the fall of 1916. They spent months strategizing, preparing, training, and stockpiling supplies leading up to the early April attack. They dug pathways underneath the German tunnels and filled them with mines that would explode. For more than a week before the battle, the Allies bombarded the ridge with over a million shells.

The battle was scheduled to begin on April 9, 1917, at 5:30 a.m. Frederick George Scott, a British priest, later wrote in his memoirs, "At five-fifteen the sky was getting lighter and already one could make out objects distinctly in the fields below. The long hand of my watch was at five-twenty-five. The fields, the roads, and the hedges were beginning to show the difference of colour in the early light. Five-twenty-seven! In three minutes the rain of death was to begin. In the awful silence around it seemed as if Nature were holding her breath in expectation of the staggering moment. Five-twenty-nine! God help our men! Five-thirty! With crisp sharp reports the iron throats of a battery nearby crashed forth their message of death to the Germans, and from three thousand guns at that moment the tempest of death swept through the air. It was a wonderful sound. The flashes of guns in all directions made lightnings in the dawn. The swish of shells through the air was continuous, and far over on the German trenches I saw the bursts of flame and smoke in a long continuous line, and, above the smoke, the white, red and green lights, which were the S.O.S. signals from the terrified enemy."

The barrage was perfectly timed so that the artillery hit and then the Canadian troops rushed in before the German soldiers had time to regroup. Canadian Corps commander Sir Julian Byng advised his troops, "Chaps, you shall go over exactly like a railroad train, on time, or you shall be annihilated." Most of the ridge was taken by noon on the first day. Harry A. Chalmers wrote in a letter, "Well it's some sight to see a battlefield after the thing is over. There is not a square inch of ground [that has not] been touched by shell fire. It's just a mess of shell holes, barb wire and torn trenches. The most awful mess I ever seen . . . The sights around the field are terrible looking. I hope I don't witness anything like it again."

Will Bird had joined the Canadian forces after the death of his brother Stephen in 1915. During the Battle of Vimy Ridge, he was sent out one night to lay barbed wire with a few other men. They didn't finish until after midnight, so they couldn't return to their trenches. Instead, they shared a small shelter known as a "bivvy" with a few

The trenches at Vimy Ridge.

soldiers from another company. He had been asleep a few hours when he felt someone pulling him out of the bivvy. He later wrote in his memoir, "In an instant I was out of the bivvy, so surprised I could not speak. I was face to face with my brother, Steve, who had been killed in 1915! . . . Steve grinned as he released my hands, then put his warm hand over my mouth as I started to shout my happiness. He pointed to the sleepers in the bivvy and to my rifle and equipment. 'Get your gear,' he said softly."

Bird grabbed his equipment and walked quickly through the sleeping troops, trying to keep pace with his brother. He ran up close and asked, "Why didn't you write Mother?" His brother replied, "Wait, don't talk yet."

Bird began to wonder how his brother had found him and why he didn't have any gear. He briefly stopped to pick up some gear he had dropped, and then he had to run to catch his brother, who was ducking into a passageway. When he got to the passageway, he couldn't see Steve. He called his brother's name, but there was no response. He searched the area but couldn't find him. So Bird sat down against a wall, figuring his brother would find him. He fell asleep.

"Suddenly I was shaken awake," Bird later wrote. "Tommy had me by the arm and was yelling. 'He's here!

Bill's here!' I stumbled up, dazed, looked at my watch. It was nine o'clock.

"'What's made you come here?' Tommy was asking. 'What happened?'

"'What's all the row about?' I countered.

"'You should know. They're digging around that bivvy you were in. All they've found is Jim's helmet and one of Bob's legs.'

"'Legs!' I echoed stupidly. 'What do you mean?'"

William Longstaff's Ghosts of Vimy Ridge.

"'Don't you know that a big shell landed in the bivvy? They've been trying to find something of you.'"

When Bird returned to the spot where he had been sleeping, he found "there was a great cavity in the embankment and debris was scattered over the whole area."

After the war was over, the French provided land on the former battlefield for the Canadian National Vimy Memorial, which is inscribed with the names of 11,285 Canadian soldiers who were listed as "missing, presumed dead" during the war. William Longstaff's 1931 painting *Ghosts of Vimy Ridge* shows the spirits of some of the brave dead on the battlefield with the monument.

10

"GOT A LIGHT?"

BATTLE OF OKINAWA, JAPAN, MAY 1945

The Battle of Okinawa was one of the last and bloodiest of World War II. A combination of US Army and Marine forces landed on the tiny Japanese island on April 1, 1945. For the next eighty-two days, it was a muddy blood-bath. Halfway through the battle, on May 7, Germany surrendered, ending the war in Europe. However, the fighting continued in the Pacific.

Marine Dale Hansen was in the thick of it on Hill 60 when, armed with a rocket launcher, he crawled over and then destroyed an enemy bunker. His rocket launcher was destroyed, so "he seized a rifle and continued his one-man assault. Reaching the crest of a ridge, he leaped across, opened fire on six Japanese and killed four before his rifle jammed. Attacked by the remaining two Japanese, he beat them off with the butt of his rifle." These heroics helped his company secure Hill 60. However, Hansen was shot and killed three days later by a Japanese sniper, never knowing that he would receive the Medal of Honor for his actions.

But this wasn't the last Okinawa would see of Private Hansen. His blood-spattered ghost would later visit the Marine camp that eventually bore his name.

☠ ☠ ☠

The small island of Okinawa, 350 miles off the coast of Japan, was essential to the United States' planned attack on the Japanese mainland. In preparation for the landing, 1,500 ships from the US Navy bombarded the beach with

World War II (1939–45) was fought between the Axis Powers (Germany, Italy, and Japan) and the Allied Powers (United States, Britain, China, Russia, and France). It was mainly fought in Europe and over the Pacific. Over 64 million people were killed, the most of any war in history.

tens of thousands of shells, rockets, and units of napalm, which burned all the plants and trees. The Japanese air force attacked these ships, sending in their kamikaze.

Crewmen fighting fires on the deck of the USS Saratoga, which was hit by Japanese kamikaze attacks off the island of Iwo Jima.

The kamikaze were a special division of the Japanese air force that flew planes packed with explosives into targets, such as ships. What made them so deadly is that the pilots of these planes planned to be killed, so they were fearless. "We didn't think too much [about dying]," Hisao Horiyama, a twenty-one-year-old Japanese kamikaze pilot, later said. "We were trained to suppress our emotions. Even if we were to die, we knew it was for a worthy cause. Dying was the ultimate fulfillment of our duty, and we were commanded not to return."

81

Ray Anderson, a sailor in the navy, remembered when one of those deadly suicide planes began to dive-bomb his ship. "Firing our guns we hit the plane so the pilot barely missed the mast of our ship . . . [He] flew about 10 feet over my head . . . exploding in the sea about 50 yards from the ship and lifting the bow of our ship partially out of the water, leaving me soaking wet from water that came over us . . . Hundreds of beautiful tropical fish floated to the surface." During the battle, waves of kamikaze killed nearly five thousand US Navy men, wounded another five thousand, sank thirty-six ships, and damaged nearly four hundred more.

On Easter Sunday, the first of more than 545,000 American troops attacked the seventy-mile-long island, expecting to have to fight the Japanese for every inch of beach. But it didn't initially happen. For a few days, the troops moved from the beaches to the interior of the lush island with little resistance.

That ended on April 6, when they reached Japanese troops waiting for them in well-fortified caves and positions that ran the width of the island. The fighting from then on was so fierce that it took the US forces nearly six weeks to advance only four miles.

Throughout the battle, it rained almost nonstop, sometimes ten inches of water in a day, turning the ground into mud. Marine William Manchester later recalled that

US forces landing on the island of Okinawa in April 1945.

the bombardment had burned away all the tropical plants, writing, "What was left resembled a cratered moonscape. But the craters were vanishing, because the rain had transformed the earth into a thin porridge—too thin even to dig foxholes [trenches for safety]. At night you lay on a poncho as a precaution against drowning during the barrages. All night, every night, shells erupted close enough to shake the mud beneath you at the rate of five or six a minute. You could hear the cries of the dying but could do nothing . . . The mud beneath our feet was deeply veined with blood. It was slippery. Blood is very slippery. So you skidded around, in deep shock, fighting as best you could."

During the nearly three-month battle, as many as one hundred thousand people who lived in Okinawa died. Many were killed by US bombs or while fighting as part of local reserve units. Many others hid in caves and refused to surrender. Zenichi Yoshimine, a child at the time, recalled, "We were taught that the Americans . . . were monsters and beasts, and not humans. So, if you were caught by them,

The marines making their way through Okinawa.

you would have your ears and nose cut off, be blinded, and be run over by the tanks." Without food and clean water, many of those hiding would die of starvation or malaria.

Many Okinawans who died in the war were students recruited to fight for the Imperial Japanese Army. Teenage boys joined what was called the Blood and Iron Imperial Corps. "We wanted to be of use to the country as quickly as we could," recalled the only survivor of a signal corps unit. "We were consumed by a burning desire to offer our lives in defense of the nation. We had no fear of death whatsoever." Female students in the Himeyuri Student Corps served as medical assistants, often dealing with terrible

The Japanese had a field hospital set up near Kadena Air Base. When the Americans took over the site, a group of nurses hid in a nearby cave. Before they could be captured, they took their own lives by blowing themselves up with grenades. Their ghosts are said to haunt the cave to this day.

wounds and amputations with little training. One of these assistants, Yoshiko Shimabukuro, later told reporters, "We only had basic training in how to put on bandages, but the wounded soldiers they brought in were beyond help. They had legs ripped off, their intestines were falling out, faces missing. We simply had no idea what to do." There were 221 students and 18 teachers of the Himeyuri Corps, with an additional 84 assigned to the medical units. By the end of the battle, 217 of them were dead.

US marine Hart Spiegel of Topeka, Kansas, tries to communicate with two Japanese child soldiers captured during the Battle of Okinawa.

After eighty-two days of fighting, the United States finally took the island on June 22, 1945. The plan originally had been to use Okinawa as a launch point to reach Japan. But the vicious battle had convinced the American government that it would be better to use the atomic bomb on Japan to end the war instead.

After World War II ended, American forces remained in Okinawa. On a dark, foggy evening in 1954, Corporal William Fetters was stationed on guard at one of the military bases. Out of the mists walked a marine, asking if Fetters had a light for his cigarette. Fetters complied and noticed blood on the man's uniform. Before he could ask what was wrong, the man turned and disappeared into the night. Though he was rattled, Fetters assumed he was just tired and was seeing things.

Weeks later, Fetters was on duty again, working with a Japanese sentry. After a rain, who came walking out of the darkness but the same marine! Again he asked, "Got a light?" before disappearing. With someone else there as a witness, Fetters knew he wasn't crazy. More sightings of the smoking marine happened over the next few months.

The next year, all the camps within the base were renamed for marines who had won the Medal of Honor.
Fetters attended the ceremony, where he recognized one of

the portraits—it was his late-night visitor! Dale Hansen, who had been so heroic during World War II, was still haunting the island a decade later.

Iwo Jima is another island that saw vicious fighting in World War II. At the battle's end, only about 1,023 of the 22,000 participating Japanese soldiers had surrendered or were taken prisoner. As many as 12,000 could only be presumed dead because their bodies have never been found. It is thought they are entombed in the underground caves where they fought. Few outside the military live on the island, and they are haunted by those ghosts. Their spirits are said to knock on doors and their ghostly faces appear in photos.

SOME FINAL THOUGHTS

Many people visit battle-fields to better imagine what happened during the wars that were fought there. They also want to pay respect to the soldiers who lost their lives. That's why visiting can be a powerful reminder of the horrors. It can also be a deterrent against going to war in the future.

As Civil War general William Tecumseh Sherman wrote, "I am tired and sick of war. Its glory is all moonshine.

General William T. Sherman

at Federal Fort No. 7.

It is only those who have neither fired a shot nor heard the shrieks and groans of the wounded who cry aloud for blood, for vengeance, for desolation. War is hell."

These battlefields are the site of so much death that it is no surprise that so many are haunted. It would be more surprising if they weren't! These poor spirits are stuck on Earth, forced to replay their terrible deaths over and over. They don't mean any harm; they just haven't accepted that they are dead.

So if you ever encounter a battlefield ghost, hope that you are the last to ever see it. These spirits deserve a little peace after so much war.

FURTHER READING

1. Demon Fire: Battle of Dan-no-ura, Japan, AD 1185
Tashiro, Osamu. *The Samurai Handbook*. Gakken, 2019.

2. Take No Prisoners: Battle of Culloden, Scotland, April 16, 1746
Strachan, Linda. *The Dangerous Lives of the Jacobites*. Kelpies, 2019.

3. Headless Horseman: Paoli Massacre, Pennsylvania, September 21, 1777
Tarshis, Lauren. *I Survived the American Revolution, 1776*. Scholastic Inc., 2017.

4. General "Mad Anthony" Wayne's Restless Ghost: Pennsylvania, December 3, 1796
Wayland, MJ. *50 Real American Ghost Stories*. Hob Hill Books, 2013.

5. Blown to Bits: Siege of Fort Erie, Canada, August 15, 1814
Raum, Elizabeth. *The Dreadful, Smelly Colonies: The Disgusting Details About Life in Colonial America*. Capstone, 2011.

6. Victory or Death!: Battle of the Alamo, Texas, March 6, 1836
Hale, Nathan. *Alamo All-Stars*. Amulet Books, 2016.

7. A Harvest of Death: Battle of Gettysburg, Pennsylvania, July 1, 1863
Tarshis, Lauren. *I Survived the Battle of Gettysburg, 1863*. Scholastic Inc., 2013.

8. Custer's Doomed Stand: Battle of Little Bighorn, Montana, June 26, 1876
Walker, Paul Robert. *Remember Little Bighorn*. National Geographic Children's Books, 2015.

9. Ghosts of the Western Front: Battle of Vimy Ridge, France, April 12, 1917
Hale, Nathan. *Treaties, Trenches, Mud, and Blood*. Amulet Books, 2014.

10. "Got a Light?": Battle of Okinawa, Japan, May 1945
Giorello, Joe. *Great Battles for Boys: WW2 in the Pacific*. Wheelhouse Publishing, 2016.

93

ACKNOWLEDGMENTS

My mom, Judy Dunn, and sisters, Heather and Jancee, have consistently given me feedback on all my writing— I am lucky to have their help. And I am also fortunate to have a terrific editor, Amanda Shih, who asks all the right questions.

Photo courtesy of Judy Dunn

Dinah Williams is an editor and children's book author who is fascinated by odd and unusual stories. Her nonfiction books for children include *Terrible But True: Awful Events in American History*; *Secrets of Walt Disney World: Weird and Wonderful Facts About the Most Magical Place on Earth*; *Abandoned Amusement Parks*; and *Spooky Cemeteries*, which won the 2009 Children's Choice Award. She lives in beautiful Cranford, New Jersey, with her husband, two daughters, and two cats, none of whom enjoys a scary story.

Don't miss more creepy stories about spooky sightings near train crashes, explosions, and floods!